# Is That You?

# WANDA M. WALKER

ISBN 979-8-88616-917-1 (paperback)
ISBN 979-8-88616-918-8 (digital)



Christian Faith Publishing
832 Park Avenue
Meadville, PA 16335
www.christianfaithpublishing.com

Printed in the United States of America

I was sewing with my head down. I was deep into the progress I was making. There wasn't anyone in the office; I was enjoying every minute of it. Suddenly, a sound that sounded like an alarm began going off. It was the most irritating sound. People in the building began leaving their offices to figure out where it was coming from. The young lady across the hall from me—whom I often say *hello* to, but as of yet, haven't gotten the chance to meet—got my attention. She too came out of the office to inquire about where the sound was coming from and what it meant? She pointed to me as she stood in the hallway looking around for answers. Then she pointed to my hair. She asked by way of suggesting with her hands, "Was it mine?"

Often, African American sisters aren't usually loaded with lots of hair unless they're mixed with another race. I assumed she was African American like me. Most of us wear weaves or braids or some sort of enhancement to our tresses. Hair takes time to manage, and super curly hair can sometimes be high maintenance. We often get help in the way of weaves and wigs. This young lady had never seen my hair puffy from the humidity. We'd had a lot that morning, this time the rain enhanced mine and made it look healthy and thick. Since I've begun the vitamins, it doesn't draw up when it rains the way it used to, so she really didn't know if it was mine naturally or mine because I paid for it.

I moved my head up and down suggesting that it was mine. She took another quick look and motioned good night as she left the building for the evening.

What she didn't know is that the mere question was a compliment. I looked down, returning back to my work, and inside my head, I smiled big. That was the first time in years someone thought my own hair was someone else's. I began thinking, *What a compliment!* What a thought! *My hair must be doing better than I thought.* Here's where my Heavenly Father comes in, "That was a first!" My pastor, recently on a Zoom call, said that we (the congregation) would experience a lot of "first-time events" before the year was out. He (God) would show Himself strong in our lives by allowing us to experience a number of "first-time events" before the year is over. I saw her comment as a first-time event. *My pastor's prophecy is coming to pass in my life already* I thought. Today was a first, and I was very excited about it.

## My Mantra

"My hair is so thick and full that I don't need a hat to keep my scalp warm in the winter."

I once met a Jewish lady on a bus in New York whose hair was so thick that I commented to her about it. She was pleasant enough to respond honestly. "Yes, my hair is very thick. It's so thick that I don't need a hat in the winter because my head never gets cold."

She didn't know it, but years later as I visualize where I wanted my hair to go, I'd repeat her words to myself with the expectation of those words producing the same results on my hair.

The next day, I went to the wig store and looked for a bust-length wig; that's the length I've always wanted for myself. At first, I thought I wanted to look at a gray or white wig, but I soon realized that it wasn't the color I was after; it was the length. So I abandoned that idea. Now I was just looking for length. There was only one that stood out, it was a very long twenty-one and a half inches, the length of the illustration I drew years ago that was posted above my bed. Each time I looked at it, I would get excited because I believed my hair would grow to that length at some point in my life; that poster drawing was an act of faith for me.

Before I made the purchase, I called my stylist and told her what I was about to do. I described the wig and its length; she suggested that I not do it. "Mrs. Wanda, it's too much hair. It's not human hair so it'll get tangled easily, and it's hard to manage. That's why I tell my customers, "Don't go so long when you're buying a wig."

I considered what she said and thought that although I detected before I left the store that it was a handful to work with, I remembered that that's the length I drew and wanted my hair to grow to, so that's the length I'm going to purchase. My reasoning was, "If I bought it, I could get accustomed to where God was taking me, this would be my trial run." I reasoned that I needed to get it; it was my assignment (LOL).

I tried it on for about five minutes in front of the store's mirror. I thought about what she said for a quick minute, thanked her on the phone, hung up, then made my purchase. I walked out of the store knowing my life was about to change.

When I got home, I immediately tried it on. It was an *unpleasant* experience. The stray hairs irritated my face. They flew all over the place. I didn't use the wig cap, so underneath the wig, my hair was loose, and that made my whole body very hot. I thought, "What have I done!" I just spent almost fifty dollars for something that doesn't look like it's gonna work. I took it off, put it down, and said, "I'll deal with that tomorrow."

Later that evening, I tried it on again and realized that bust length hair is a responsibility. It's synthetic, so it really does tangle easily. It has a certain weight to it that makes it hot and heavy on my head, and I don't think it reacts well to moisture or rain. Now if I'd grown it naturally, I would've had time to adjust to the weight over time but because it wasn't a gradual process, I was bothered by all the problems it caused.

Emotionally, something was happening to me; I could feel it. I was in unfamiliar waters; I knew I was supposed to learn something if I saw this all the way through. But would I? It was starting to feel uncomfortable. This was a very different route for me; normally, when I've seen people with wigs this length, I always thought negative thoughts of them. *How superficial you are! What's all that length about? Are they trying to be another race? One that has naturally long hair?* (I secretly believed only White, Orientals, Hispanic, and Indian people had long hair, and that's because I'd never met anyone of African descent with bust-length hair; I had limited exposure.) That doesn't mean they're not out there; I just never met them.

The mere act of wearing a wig made me face bias issues that were in me, and they were all negative. I found myself judgmental of other women. I felt that they didn't have the right to wear something fake and call it real. Then I wondered, *But who gave me the right to judge them?* I found that mindset in me very disturbing. Having all this hair on my head forced me to confront all my bias about women and their standard of beauty. I thought, *Come on ladies, do you really need all that to prove something?* I could clearly see I had issues with hair and what it meant to me. I'd never seen that before in me.

It was awful. I felt a shame come over me because of what I detected in me; it wasn't very pretty. The real shock was that the things I'd thought about others, I was afraid others would now think about me, and that made me very uncomfortable. The guns were turned on me. I'd never expressed this to another person; it was a secret, even to me. I'd never really examined it before. Now it was in my face, and I had to look at it.

It's Saturday evening, and I've tried it on again. I looked in the mirror in my own home, and I began sweating while I was standing there trying it out. It's tight on my head. I took a selfie and sent it to one person whose opinion I respected, and the other person was a cousin of mine and a big wig wearer, meaning, she wore wigs as a regular thing. I wanted to know what their thoughts were.

They were shocked and didn't know what to say. To be honest, it didn't look all that great on me, and they may have seen what I saw, but they didn't want to insult me, so they said very little. They both tried to be polite, but it was evident that they didn't know what to say because it wasn't a fabulous look for me.

By calling them, I was testing it and trying to get a feel for how others would react to me in it. I was trying to prepare myself for what I felt would come. But what I was really feeling was the embarrassment of believing the lie that others who wore wigs didn't feel good about themselves. That they were less of a person.

My religious upbringing ridiculed women who wore them. It judged them as not being holy or spiritual. I believed that if you wanted long hair, you should grow it, but you shouldn't buy it. And now I bought it. What was I to do? I'd contradicted myself and done what I said I didn't believe in. I was embarrassed to look at myself. And I'd bought it because my Father indicated that this was a remedy for me in an area that I'd suffered in for *forty* years. What I didn't know was that I had held myself in prison and I was about to be released from captivity.

Standing in front of the mirror wearing it didn't make it any easier to wear. I imagined how I would have to wear this to work on Monday. It was Saturday night, and I just couldn't see that! I took it off, but it troubled me all night. I dreaded Monday morning coming, but I knew that it would.

Sunday came, and after my zoom church service, I put the wig on to wear around the house. I imagined wearing it was a part of the healing remedy for Alopecia (A condition some have that prevents them from growing hair in some spots. In serious cases people don't grow hair anywhere on their bodies). In my early twenties, I had a verbal fight with a relative, and the next day, I woke up with a bald spot on the back of my head the size of a nickel. That became a condition, and it formed a pattern.

After that, I noticed that whenever I got stressed about anything, my emotional state was reflective in my hair. It would shed. When I was at peace, it grew. My emotional state controlled it. In short, I was affected by worry and fear; two cousins our lord tells us to stay clear of. He said in John 14:1, "Let not your heart be troubled." Clearly, things troubled me; and when my hair fell out because of it, I become more troubled.

Just by putting the wig on my head, I was addressing issues in me. Somehow, God was melting them away. On one level I believed that wearing it gave me the faith to believe that I could grow hair that length. On another level, I carried shame for feeling that I needed to wear it.

Growing hair isn't an impossibility, because with God, all things are possible, what I'm addressing here is my *need* to grow it, to have it, to be seen by others with it, and the security that it created for me.

For many years, I reasoned that pursuing it was my stretch of faith, but making that the issue, helped me to avoid the real issue, which were feelings of inadequacy. Now that I had the hair, I realized that long hair, human hair, real, or synthetic wasn't the issue, the issue was self-acceptance (accepting myself). It was my inability to accept myself as I was. Why was accepting myself so difficult? What was wrong with me? Was there anything wrong with me? Was I so different from other people? What was really going on inside of me, and why did my hair make *all* the difference? I needed to stop worrying, to accept myself, to love myself, and to trust that my Father had made me well regardless of the length of my hair. Hair had no bearing on who He made me to be.

He said in Genesis 1:26 that He chose to make me, then in verse 1:27 he said that I was created in His image, and in 1:28 he said that He blessed me and gave me work, He told me to be fruitful, fruitful in the gifts he'd given me—develop them, multiply them, increase them, and expand them. I had talent and ability in other areas—why was I stuck on hair? And more importantly, Why was having it so very important to me? Up until this point, I'd done everything I knew to grow it; and although it was growing at a normal pace, I didn't understand my obsession with it. I wanted to get to the root of it. Was it God leading me? Was I leading myself? I just knew I had to bring it to a close. Enough was enough! He showed confidence in the ability He'd given me; I was like Him and made in His image. He'd given me His tools; His thinking capacity to work with. He'd created me to think like Him, to be creative and make witty inventions, with sound reasoning, surely, I was enough. Why did I need hair to feel a sense of self-worth? Clearly, something was out of order. The self-inspection brought out the negative thoughts I'd buried deep. While looking for answers for one thing, I found unfounded negative bias beliefs that weren't supported by anything in other areas. I found beliefs with no backup and no substance. It was time to lay them all down and rebuild my core—find it.

God cleaned out some really negative thinking about people in me. Now I could see what He was doing with me, wearing it became a must because wearing it helped me to see the negative attitude in me and that had to be dealt with.

# Monday Morning Came

As I was showering, I heard Joel Olsteen say something on my dresser radio that encouraged me to step out and wear the new wig. Before I turned him on, I had already decided to "not" wear it that day. I'd already done my hair, and I was about to walk out the door for work. I talked myself out of it and released myself of the discomfort I felt all weekend. But once I heard his message, I returned to the bathroom mirror and put it on again. It was scary, but it was something I felt that I had to do.

It was uncomfortable. Once again, the hairs got in my way. I couldn't put my head down without it touching my lip gloss and sticking to it. Fine hair on my lips, ucky! It got in my eyes and blocked my vision. I quickly understood why people who wore wigs that length also pinned the sides down (which I always thought defeated the whole purpose of such extravagant hair). But now, I noticed that without the pins to hold it back, it could be very irritating on your face. I considered abandoning my dream of growing hair that length simply because of what I was experiencing that morning. It was awful. But that was progress.

I stepped outside to put something in the car. I heard someone from across the street (it sounded like my neighbor). One neighbor hollered to the other neighbor, "Hey, Bobby." (another person on the street), "Bobby, come. Come now! Bobby, come right now!" I swore he was referring to me! He was probably saying, "Come and look at the lady across the street (me) in her new wig." No one said that, but it felt like that to me.

I ignored it because I had to. This was a monumental moment, and I had to own it and take the challenge. I got the rest of my things that I needed for the day, closed my front door behind me, locked it, got in my car, and drove off to work.

Once I got to work, I parked and sat inside for a moment. I kept wondering if I could do it. Could I get out of the car in this wig? *I've got to. I've got to see this all the way through.* So I did. I walked in the front door and passed the security person. He looked at me as I passed by. I could feel his eyes looking, but I wouldn't meet his gaze. When he last saw me on Thursday of the previous week, I had gray and white hair, now it was black and very long. What could I say? Nothing. I passed him and got on the elevator.

A gentleman and I rode up together. I asked him how his weekend was? He turned to answer and quickly turned away. You know the look you take of someone on the street who's dressed strangely? You look at them and wonder, *How did they manage to leave the house looking like that?* I knew I must have had that look; like the comedian Lily Tomlin on the seventy's television comedy show "Laugh In." She wore that funny little black hair net with a knot in the middle of her forehead. She looked so ridiculous that when you looked at her, you just had to laugh. I had the uncut mesh that wigs come with these days to make them look like your own hair. It's a piece of flesh-color fabric that the wigs are made on. The manufacturers extend the fabric beyond the scalp area and into your forehead. It's there so the buyer can customize it and cut along the hairline once you decide where you want it. You're supposed to cut the mesh down very close to the wig's hairline so that it looks like you're growing it right out of your scalp. I hadn't cut mine down. I wore it with that piece hanging from it. I knew you were supposed to cut it, a customer in the wig store told me, but I wasn't sure if I was going to return it to the store, and I knew that if I did, I'd better return it the way I purchased it. Mine was almost exactly my skin tone, so I reasoned that it blended with my skin, and no one would notice it. *Wrong!* The gentleman on the elevator did. Plus, my issue wasn't to make it look natural, my issue was to wear it.

Once he turned to look at me and then quickly turned away, he answered my question. I imagine he was embarrassed for me. If he wasn't, I was. While my insides were very nervous, I maintained a conversation as if nothing was wrong.

The next hurdle was to see Undra, my boss.

I walked down the hall toward my office hot and sweaty but relieved that it was almost over. I'd worn it. Now I only had to explain it to her. Or so I thought. When I got to the office, I noticed she hadn't come yet. Thank God!

I put my key in the door, and immediately, the *weight was lifted off my shoulders*! I had broken through something! Some kind of barrier or hindrance. Some kind of invisible obstruction. All the anxiety I had about it lifted! Suddenly, I felt free and very light. I'd done it! Whatever it was that kept me from enjoying my own hair and not accepting myself was gone, and it was no longer an issue. Wearing it outside among people for one day broke chains off of me! Whatever it was that held me bound, no longer had me. I was free!

Now that I'm free, I've rethought the whole hair idea. For the first time in my life, I don't think I need all that hair. This is an astonishing conclusion to me. What's happening to me? Now it seemed like a huge unnecessary bother to maintain. The luster of it all wore off. Now I just wanted to get through whatever I was going through. With all of what I'd experience that weekend, I was finish with the long hair dream. I now saw it in a whole new light, and I wasn't impressed by it. It was bothersome.

I thought I could use it as a witness tool, but now I just didn't want it for anything. Going public with my thoughts about how it exposed something extremely ugly in me hurt, it was revealing, but I was glad I saw it. It was embarrassing. Did I really need that? Was it really necessary? After forty years of pursuing it, I must have thought that I wasn't enough and hair added to me.

# End of the Day

U ndra came in at 10:00 a.m. By that time, I'd put it on the mini-ironing board beside my sewing machine. I waited for the middle of the day to explain what I was doing with it. She never noticed it. When I brought it to her attention. Her response was, "It's just hair." It wasn't an issue for her, and I understood that. From the looks of things, it was no longer my issue either. It was just too much. Quietly, I'd given it up and returned to a normal life; one that had nothing to do with hair. For so many years, that was all I dreamt of. Now I was free.

I didn't really see the freedom until I told my friend from my church OMC about the entire ordeal I'd been through. She suggested that I had to go through it. I had to face what was in me in order to rid myself of it. She could be right. I never thought of it that way, but now I was free, and it felt wonderful.

These days, I don't want to think about hair. I like my own, and I'm happy that I don't have to have a lap full. I'm happy knowing that that's behind me. I'll grow it naturally, and I'll enjoy whatever it does, but I'm not going after it anymore. I'm not even going to look at wigs again. I'm tired of it all. Each time I look in the mirror, I enjoy what I see. Me! Wherever it goes, that's where it goes; I'm not pursuing it. It had a hold on me for forty years, and now I'm over it.

I may never share this story with anyone or maybe with everyone. One thing is for sure, I never want to spend my day thinking about the existence of the one thing that will make or break me. I am fearfully and wonderfully made in the image of my Father. I am a unique individual with or without hair. I have value and substance, and I am the apple of my Father's eye. When He formed me in my mother's womb, he gave me purpose and status; my external appearance meets with His approval. I am enough. Long, short, or no hair will not add to my value because I am whole and complete in Him.

There's a battle that's still going on inside my walls—it's the fight to be free of the opinion of others. These days, I'm fighting to value myself in my own eyes. The way I go about it is to not *need or seek* the external approval of others but rather to approve myself.

When I do a job of any sort, I gauge whether or not I did a good job by my results and intentions. Recently, I've made a note of not asking others for their approval of my work. I know when I've done my best at something and when I've thrown it together. I don't need anyone to point out whether or not the job is good when deep down (and not even so deep) inside I know when I've done my best.

These days, I want to do my best in everything. It's not always the best, but it's my best; and I give all I have in anything I do. I haven't always done that, but I do now. Now, the reward is better.

Living without the approval of others isn't easy. I've found myself hanging out on the fence longer than I want to because I'm judging my intentions and my goal in everything. I'm looking for the integrity in everything I do. It's a bit harder but clearly a lot more rewarding. It's nice not needing the approval of others. It's liberating. Some days, I feel like I'm walking down the street naked—that's because I'm so accustom to being a people pleaser; that's how I lived most of my previous life. Now, I check the intentions of my heart. If it lines up with the word of God, I'll go forward. If it doesn't, I'll stop and check my intentions. I do a lot of stopping and a lot of about facing. I believe that will change in time. It's all good. I understand myself better now. I love and accept myself. It's no longer the hair anymore; it's the intentions of the heart.

Quietly contemplating my new look.

The author of this book has opened up a conversation about self-acceptance. Often, people attribute this to be a women's topic, but it can be an issue for both men and women, young and old. Anyone can benefit from this conversation and grow.

She has confronted deep-seated private views that she held. They reflected a negative view of herself without her having full knowledge of it. She painted a horrific view of others that was equally as crippling. Then one day, she was suddenly confronted with her dark side and realized she had to make an about-face. Lost and frightened, she turned to her Heavenly Father, and cried out for help to change. Take a look at how her view of herself all unfolded in the process of four days.